GW00498768

Handling

Jack Thacker grew up on a farm in Herefordshire. He recently completed a PhD on contemporary poetry at the Universities of Bristol and Exeter. His poetry has been published in many print and online magazines and has been broadcast on Radio 4. He was the winner of the 2016 Charles Causley International Poetry Competition and the poet-in-residence at the Museum of English Rural Life at the University of Reading from October 2017 to March 2018.

Also by Two Rivers poets

David Attwooll, *The Sound Ladder* (2015)

Kate Behrens, *The Beholder* (2012)

Kate Behrens, *Man with Bombe Alaska* (2016)

Adrian Blamires, *The Pang Valley* (2010)

Adrian Blamires & Peter Robinson (eds.), *The Arts of Peace* (2014)

David Cooke, *A Murmuration* (2015)

Terry Cree, *Fruit* (2014)

Claire Dyer, *Eleven Rooms* (2013)

Claire Dyer, *Interference Effects* (2016)

John Froy, *Sandpaper & Seahorses* (2018)

A. F. Harrold, *The Point of Inconvenience* (2013)

Ian House, *Nothing's Lost* (2014)

Gill Learner, *The Agister's Experiment* (2011)

Gill Learner, *Chill Factor* (2016)

Sue Leigh, *Chosen Hill* (2018)

Becci Louise, *Octopus Medicine* (2017)

Mairi MacInnes, *Amazing Memories of Childhood, etc.* (2016)

Steven Matthews, *On Magnetism* (2017)

Henri Michaux, *Storms under the Skin* translated by Jane Draycott (2017)

Tom Phillips, *Recreation Ground* (2012)

John Pilling & Peter Robinson (eds.), *The Rilke of Ruth Speirs:*
  New Poems, Duino Elegies, Sonnets to Orpheus & Others (2015)

Peter Robinson, *English Nettles and Other Poems* (2010)

Peter Robinson (ed.), *Reading Poetry: An Anthology* (2011)

Peter Robinson (ed.), *A Mutual Friend: Poems for Charles Dickens* (2012)

Peter Robinson, *Foreigners, Drunks and Babies: Eleven Stories* (2013)

Lesley Saunders, *Cloud Camera* (2012)

Lesley Saunders, *Nominy-Dominy* (2018)

Robert Seatter, *The Book of Snow* (2016)

Susan Utting, *Fair's Fair* (2012)

Susan Utting, *Half the Human Race* (2017)

Jean Watkins, *Scrimshaw* (2013)

Handling

Jack Thacker grew up on a farm in Herefordshire. He recently completed a PhD on contemporary poetry at the Universities of Bristol and Exeter. His poetry has been published in many print and online magazines and has been broadcast on Radio 4. He was the winner of the 2016 Charles Causley International Poetry Competition and the poet-in-residence at the Museum of English Rural Life at the University of Reading from October 2017 to March 2018.

Also by Two Rivers poets

David Attwooll, *The Sound Ladder* (2015)

Kate Behrens, *The Beholder* (2012)

Kate Behrens, *Man with Bombe Alaska* (2016)

Adrian Blamires, *The Pang Valley* (2010)

Adrian Blamires & Peter Robinson (eds.), *The Arts of Peace* (2014)

David Cooke, *A Murmuration* (2015)

Terry Cree, *Fruit* (2014)

Claire Dyer, *Eleven Rooms* (2013)

Claire Dyer, *Interference Effects* (2016)

John Froy, *Sandpaper & Seahorses* (2018)

A. F. Harrold, *The Point of Inconvenience* (2013)

Ian House, *Nothing's Lost* (2014)

Gill Learner, *The Agister's Experiment* (2011)

Gill Learner, *Chill Factor* (2016)

Sue Leigh, *Chosen Hill* (2018)

Becci Louise, *Octopus Medicine* (2017)

Mairi MacInnes, *Amazing Memories of Childhood, etc.* (2016)

Steven Matthews, *On Magnetism* (2017)

Henri Michaux, *Storms under the Skin* translated by Jane Draycott (2017)

Tom Phillips, *Recreation Ground* (2012)

John Pilling & Peter Robinson (eds.), *The Rilke of Ruth Speirs: New Poems, Duino Elegies, Sonnets to Orpheus & Others* (2015)

Peter Robinson, *English Nettles and Other Poems* (2010)

Peter Robinson (ed.), *Reading Poetry: An Anthology* (2011)

Peter Robinson (ed.), *A Mutual Friend: Poems for Charles Dickens* (2012)

Peter Robinson, *Foreigners, Drunks and Babies: Eleven Stories* (2013)

Lesley Saunders, *Cloud Camera* (2012)

Lesley Saunders, *Nominy-Dominy* (2018)

Robert Seatter, *The Book of Snow* (2016)

Susan Utting, *Fair's Fair* (2012)

Susan Utting, *Half the Human Race* (2017)

Jean Watkins, *Scrimshaw* (2013)

Handling

Jack Thacker

*For Chris
with Thanks

Jack Thacker*

TWO
RIVERS
PRESS

First published in the UK in 2018 by Two Rivers Press
7 Denmark Road, Reading RG1 5PA
www.tworiverspress.com

ISBN 978-1-909747-43-2

1 2 3 4 5 6 7 8 9

Two Rivers Press is represented in the UK by Inpress Ltd
and distributed by NBNi.

Cover design by Nadja Guggi using a photograph of the plaster-cast hands
of Joseph Arch
Text design by Nadja Guggi and typeset in Janson and Parisine

Printed and bound in Great Britain by Imprint Digital, Exeter

In Memory of John Thacker

1927–2018

Acknowledgements

Acknowledgements are due to the editors of the following, where some of these poems, a few in earlier versions, first appeared: *The Literateur*, *The Looking Glass Anthology* (University of York), and *Buildings of Nature* (Creative Arts Anthology, University of Reading). 'The Load' won first prize in the 2016 Charles Causley International Poetry Competition.

The poems in Part II arose out of a residency undertaken at the Museum of English Rural Life at the University of Reading from October 2017 to March 2018, funded by the Arts and Humanities Research Council through the South West and Wales Doctoral Training Partnership. I am grateful to each and every member of staff at the museum. Special thanks go to: Kate Arnold-Forster, Guy Baxter, Caroline Benson, Mat Binks, Ollie Douglas, Danielle Eade, Jen Glanville, Caroline Gould, Phillippa Heath, Alison Hilton, Isabel Hughes, Adam Koszary, Naomi Lebens, Adam Lines, Ceri Lumley, Timothy Jerrome and Rhi Smith.

I am grateful to Peter Robinson for his guidance as an editor, to Sally Mortimore for the book's production and to Nadja Guggi for its design. Further thanks go to Martin Lloyd and Annie Murray, who kindly took me on as their own domestic poet-in-residence during my time at Reading, to my family for their inspiration, to Rachel Murray for keeping me grounded, and to everyone else who gave encouragement, feedback and support.

Contents

Part I

Handling

A low, slow burn, early summer sun
dyes the evening orange, through barn slats
casts lines on broom-swept stone.

They lay out boards that shine
with wax, oil and string up shears
from an oak beam, support their backs.

My job is to handle the ewes,
to catch them in the pen and guide them
within reach of the shearers.

But their gated frames are too huge
for my span of arms, their sinewy legs
too strong, too stubborn –

no effort of mine can hurdle their will.
It's not until Dad takes over
and I have time between rolling fleeces

to watch him, that I understand
the placement of a knee, the gentle rock
of a heel at the opportune moment.

The Cabbage Planter

The sky spilt its ink in clear water.
We headed for the veg-patch bearing trays
of leeks, white cabbage, savoy, winter
greens. You were waiting on bare clay

that you'd worked to a fine grain,
tractor running, cabbage-planter raised:
a desk of seedlings, three rusty thrones
where we'd sit and work together side by side.

This time it was my turn to guide us
down the row, to hold a straight line.
You showed me the gears, adjusted the wheel,

then, before a quick 'mind your fingers',
shut the cab: a thud, a pulsing pain,
a black cloud in the sunset of my nail.

Exchange

Together we went out into the storm
to tend to a beast that was dying:
a survivor of pneumonia, the weather
too severe for its weakened lungs.
I opened the gate to the paddock
and you crept in with the loader.
We could see the hunk of silhouette:

its stomach was blown – its fate sealed –
and glistened like a flesh balloon
in a lightning flash. You tied a rope
around its hoof, as its bowels –
preparing for death – emptied.
I grabbed the sticky cord and pulled
while you scooped with hydraulics …

Out there, we were two trawler men
on some lonely North Sea vessel,
hauling from the deep a loaded net
while wind and rain and spray
lashed across our fingers and faces.
Finally, the bucket swallowed its load
with the dignity of dumped cargo.

We drove home blind with the calf
in front, spot-lit, floating above
the ground, its hooves pointing up.
Under cover in the barn, you slid it
onto the straw and its body made
the sound of a bathtub draining.
Its eyes had sunk inside its head,

its tongue swollen in its jaw.
'I should put it down', you said,
'but tonight I don't have the heart.'
'At least it will die in the warm,'
I replied. That night, our cat –
missing for days now – at last
came in injured from the storm.

October

A jackdaw's crumb falls from the chimney
landing on the boards at our feet.
Meanwhile, a leaf's skeleton dries
as the house emits tectonic groans
and rooms that lie on the peripheries
are left to die in the cold.

Outside, bedouin sheep migrate
trailing arteries in the grass;
the dog sits like a used mop in the yard
waiting for the coal to arrive,
while through gales and broken yells,
finally, the cattle come home.

Turning In

The pestle of hoof-butts on gravel, the bulk
of flank and barrel as the cattle stumble
on towards their winter keep, guided on
either side by hurdles, gestures of fence,
goaded from behind, the family in a line,
the farmyard a funnel, destined for the barn.

They pour onto straw in the rush of a wave
on shore, a cloud of fantail sparking chaff.
They kick and hurl and churn but safe –
we're tying gates, standing in the gap.

The Stick

Not a solid staff of hazel
nor a personal rod of holly
carefully sculpted and fluted by ivy
with a practical V and emblazoned initial

but a grabbed-in-a-flash half-yard
length of blue piping, bent slightly
so, if swung in the wind,
it catches the air and whistles very faintly.

Pipes

Walking after rain in the treeless
orchard, I feel my footsteps
cast ripples below a surface
of grass. Each impact comes up
again as the sound of roasting
oil. At the edge of the forest,
the whirr of pheasants roosting,
clearing their throats in unrest.

Later, I stand at the kitchen
sink with my mother and a brace
of pheasants. She says 'press
there, on the chest of the hen' –
I listen intent for the hiss
as air is pumped from its breast.

Polishing the Brass

In Memoriam T.M.R., 1917–2012

When the family dispersed
after the Sunday roast –
son-in-law working fields,
daughter chatting with friends,
the children busy playing –
you could be found polishing
the horse-brass in the cool
and quiet dining room,
newspaper laid out square
on the table, and there
all afternoon you'd dip
your can of Brasso and rub
until each piece shone.

Now that you've gone
the brass is packed away,
but in the calm of each Sunday
the scent of ammonia,
the plaques laid out on paper
and you alone and at peace
hanging them in place.

Turn

Earth rose up from the tractor's prow
like a cresting wave; behind
was turned into lines in the plough's
wake. Four hands made ground

as I declined the banks of the valley,
reciting the words we'd rehearsed
together on the lip of the gully:
clutch/brake, *wheel-turn*, *reverse*.

Were you watching from the window
as I wove my yarn across the field,
wondering each time I went down
below the tree line if I'd found

the pedal? Waiting for my signal –
a flash of sun on polished steel.

The Load

Listening to your recording
crackle away like kindling,
my mind becomes the barn:
the sun reaches in through

a single door, the floor –
years' worth of dry muck
and straw – is kicked and
raised to dust by the strut

of cloven hooves; and when,
from out of the shadows,
your voice arrives, I can
hear the scream of the bull

echoing along the beams,
glimpse its shuddering hide
through gaps in the steam.
Standing on the threshold

the others are shaking their
heads. That's when you –
when you were sixteen –
vault the gate and stride

towards the tonne of stress
and muscle. I can read
the surprise on their faces
as you reach out your hand

and loop your finger through
its nose-ring – so easy –
like I might thread a
cassette-tape with a pencil,

winding back the spool
to listen again to you
as you calmly lead the bull
away and into the light.

Part II

Museum Pieces

i. Diary

Looking again at what's been handed to me:
Young Mr Peter Pownall's Farm Diary
in letters tattooed crudely on hardened goatskin.

Its pages are fungal: dark as the gills of a flat cap,
mud-flecked as shirt cuffs, frail as a folded map.
The paper itself holds notes of rain on dust.

One-line entries for each day, that's all
he allowed for himself, the farmer Pownall.
A life and times summed up with few spare words.

17th October: 'Killed two hives of bees';
4th November: 'Thomas Shacroft was Burriid
and died of it'; 14th: 'Thatched bee Hives.'

ii. Skep

I don white gloves and peer into the skep –
the whole thing looks wet like a greasy crop,
its dandruff of dry straw shedding everywhere.

The inside still smells faintly of wax.
A layer of filth reminds me of crusted cattle muck.
I notice the label reads: 'livestock, bees'.

Death is sweet – that's something you learn
young on a farm. Tiny pieces of honeycomb
have dried to a crisp and turned black as scabs.

I imagine the young Pownall: digging a pit,
lighting brimstone, placing the hive above it,
waiting – a low hum fading in strength.

Put Your Hands Together

Joseph Arch (1826–1919)

The crows soon grow wise
to the strength of his throwing arm.
He claps his hands, they glide
(reflecting in the dark of his eyes)
to the far side of the field.
It's a kind of game
and crows don't get tired.
Arch is nine years old:
bird-scarer, wage-earner, child.

He cups a nest in his palm
that hours later is thrashed –
the price for a wayward mind.
So, he turns his hand
to mouldboard, coulter, beam,
scratching away at the land.
At thirteen, he's driving a team.
All day Arch is pushed
and, falling short, he's punished.

Retreating inside his head,
at night he eagerly reads:
the Bible, Shakespeare, a paper
purchased out-of-date.
One day, he asks his master
to try his prentice hand
at becoming a new-styled hedge-cutter.
It works, increases his rate.
Body and mind are sound.

With his reputation growing
as mower, hedger and ditcher,
in all his hours to spare
he thinks on the farm-worker's problem.
He finds himself a wife
who raises seven offspring:
'six of whom are still living',
he writes at the end of his life.
Soon his time will come.

1872, February:
three men come to the door
wanting to start a union.
That night, a meeting in Wellesbourne –
Arch speaks for an hour
under a chestnut tree
to an audience of two thousand
gathered from miles around.
The word's been passed on.

Under a full moon shining
everyone stays out listening,
hoisting up lanterns on bean poles –
nobody wanders off.
Distribution should undo excess,
and each man have enough,
quotes Arch, on a pig-killing stool.
The meeting's a success –
the first stirrings of progress.

It stays long in his mind
this image of rural England:
faces with dark about them.
It forms the perfect hailstorm.
From the tree in Wellesbourne
branches reach out everywhere.
He travels from shire to shire,
speaks – the people answer,
rise from valleys of bones.

Together they strike as one
but are met with the bite of frost,
the dead hand of the church,
the farmer's arbitrary fist.
At the centre there's Arch
holding it all together:
'put heart into each other,'
he tells the men of the union
starving inside their skin.

Others say he's wrong
and seek to do him harm
but he knows well the saying:
'threatened men live long.'
Later, union in fragments,
he carries it on by standing:
'Order, the bird-scarer's speaking.
No clapping in Parliament!'
Retires to his childhood home.

No death mask for him – hands,
the hands of a farm labourer.
Or is that former labourer
turned unioniser, preacher?
They lie, holding a pen,
in case his cause be forgotten,
gone through time as through blackthorn
so all his scars can be seen –
each a mark on the land.

Orphan Work

'Woman with Ivy', Minnie Jane Hardman

Everything about her is silver: 'second-place',
'graphite on paper'. Her hair and her eyes
are a deeper shade; her neck and her face –
surface hardly touched. An exercise.

Still, there are signs of a solitary skill:
the softness of feature, the ear, the frill
of the delicate pleated collar, that small
subtle dimple in the chin, and the non-smile

rendered (familiar to those who knew her).
Untraceable. They call her an 'orphan work',
says the curator. Twisted on her shoulder

is ivy or 'bindwood' or 'lovestone', a mark
of bonds and of worth, green in winter –
it thrives in the wild, the frozen, the dark.

While the Earth Remaineth

Wilfred Fisher Wyatt (1937)

Picture a Samuel Palmer come to life –
the resin run, freeing limb, the sky
opening: a parting cloud (even in sepia
sunlight bleaches the ground). The earth, a wave
breaks on itself. Booted footsteps following.

'First the blade, and then the ear, Then –.'

A whispering in the corn, a ticking. A reaper
turning, turning. This one, sharpening, painting
his blade thin. This one, gathering sheaves,
tying them – now glancing towards the camera –
a bundle in each arm, leaning, stooking.

'To the next field.'

Horses, three abreast. The dog wanders
behind. Here he is, with his best mates,
coupling to the machine. He stops, strokes their ears,
looking up at the camera: in close up. Here
they stand, the horses grazing. A moment. Cut.

'Leading'

Impossible. A wagon stacked like a cloud
in the evening light: a last load, swaying
top-heavy through the gate. Everyone smiling,
riding high or walking lightly – except
the horses struggling – uphill towards the house.

'On the Wolds'

Pitching: a pole vault perfect pitch of a fork –
father and son, unloading back at the barn,
the old man, his spine bent, arching into
a hillock. Still he works as hard – harder
than anyone – though blinkered now to the ground.

'Off again'

No-one's catching the eye of the camera today –
everyone's stares at the other novel machine.
A movable barn, and inside: pure light.
One by one, they hold out their palm and run
through fingers processed time.

'The End.'

Foot and Mouth

Dir. Lindsay Anderson (1955)

A farm somewhere in England, sometime
in Autumn. This is Bury Farm,
its crops, livestock (soon to be buried).
It's November now. How to read
the signs but not commit yourself –
leave that to officials. For this calf,
too late. The whole thing's deadly efficient:
a touch / a tyre / a train / a footprint.

The poetry survives. It's not in the voice
explaining protocol, it lies in the face
of a woman watching (shots off-screen) –
shot of a herd, of a vet, of a gun,
shot of an empty field on a hill,
shot of a farmer shot of it all.

Forceps

I'm struggling to get my head round it:

how did they make it
                    all that way
from maternity ward
to lambing shed?

                    And how did they feel,
those ribbons of steel
on the rat-like skull
                    of a lamb?

Hands
        fashioned to cradle
                            life
in the round –
                'Pull, pull it now.'

'The hooks won't hold.'
'They will. They'll hold. It's coming ...'

Galleries

Strip lights, white walls, transparencies.
A place for implements after they die.

It feels halfway like returning home,
so it's easy to imagine the forgotten

corners or verges of a yard where
nettles and tall grass harboured these shapes.

Trappings of a craft and cast-off tools
tell the truth: all farms are graveyards.

*

In the background, storm clouds break
but things remain at peace in here;

objects stand in relief, speaking only
of themselves. The layout, minimal.

With all this white space to soil, I think,
the mess they'd leave behind if cattle

came this way, with us driving them
in rain
            through the gate to our yard.

*

Whitewashed walls: the blank of a page.

Write it now, whatever comes to mind
as long as it stays in your head, or leave
a few lines in the visitor's book.

Yet sometimes it's hard to articulate
the sense of an object lost somewhere

in the middle of it all – a means
to what end? The meaning. The end.

                            *

You walk on, turning a corner, when
a room takes form before your eyes
have time to adjust and you remember
where you are –
                            steam from saucepans
rises, misting glass;
                            the door opens
and everyone gathers around the table –
except
            it's unclear:
                            are you there
or here,
            sitting
                            or looking down?

                            *

Participant observation –

                           writing not
from the outside in, like a stranger who's
made themselves known and familiar

but from inside out: to be your own
ethnographer.

                   But what of the people
this is all about? Was it given?

Repeat his words again: *the self
is only interesting as an illustration.*

                    *

I beeline for the Herefordshire wagon
('small but sturdy' sounds about right) –

bowed as a boat, dried out as driftwood
there it stands, somehow still bracing

from a lifetime of loads, the strain of horses
in harvest, and the tractor that pulled it
up to '56, its wheels like buckled knees.

Too late for them to spring back now.

                    *

Can you help it, betraying your debts?
How would he have managed it?

(The other one I mean, the one who
followed.) What might he have felt?

A museum of English rural life:
it would have been a discomfort, I imagine.

And yet, might he have gleaned in the straw-
or the basket-work something green?

                              *

Everywhere you turn
                              you're reflecting
on yourself: now your torso's wicker;
now your arms are tools,
                              your head
caught in a trap.
                    Always your image
masks a clear view. A part of you
is mirrored in each familiar artefact.

A cabinet of glass, a figure inside,
about your height; a wax jacket, worn.

                              *

Now and again, a patient comes by
from the hospital over the road, guided
in wheelchair by son, daughter or carer.

And yes, it's right, I think to myself,

they're side by side: a place of life
and death, a museum of rural life.

They take their time, then quietly
                              slip away
back to the lights and hum of the ward.

Afterword

For nearly a decade now I've been writing poems about my experiences growing up on a small farm in Herefordshire. More recently, I've been exploring the complicated and ancient relationship between poetry and agriculture (it goes deeper than you might think) in an academic context. It was during my studies that I first encountered the Museum of English Rural Life in Reading. By the time I had departed the museum on the day of that first visit, the idea of a poetry residency – which would eventually lead to this book – was already firmly in place.

As it happens, the MERL is the perfect place in which to indulge in the twin passions of research and writing – not to mention a passion for rural life itself. In its very layout, the building encourages intellectual discovery and hands-on experience in equal measure. Its archives contain countless treasures, among them the remarkable diary of Peter Pownall, featured here in the poem 'Museum Pieces'. It was in the museum's reading room that I would learn about eighteenth-century beekeeping practices, which seem cruel by modern standards. It was there that I would also read about how Pownall would thatch his beehives (skeps) to protect them from the weather. The proximity of the archives to the galleries, as well as the accessibility of the museum's open stores, meant that all I had to do to get a better sense of these objects was talk to curator Ollie Douglas and I was able to handle examples of them myself.

If the reading room was where I cultivated a deeper understanding of rural history, the galleries prompted me to contemplate my own. I'll never forget walking around them for the very first time and recognising so many objects that were familiar to me from our family farm as it exists today. Except in this case (and in each glass case) the trappings and tools of a way of life I knew so well were on display to the public, in a kind of stasis. The shock of this made me think: was my own farm a living museum? On numerous occasions I've found myself performing a double take at the mannequins featured in certain displays, for sometimes I could have sworn I caught a glimpse of my parents.

The poems in part I of *Handling* are taken from a larger body of work based on personal experience. Part II was written over the period of the six-month residency and each poem relates to a specific object from the galleries or an item (or film footage) from the archives. The final poem is an account of the uncanny experience of exploring the galleries themselves.

Notes

Museum Pieces

i. Diary
The Diary of Young Mr Peter Pownall (MERL FR CHE 1/1/1).
Peter Pownall (1765–1858) was a farmer who lived in Bramall
in Cheshire.

ii. Skep
A skep is an old-fashioned beehive made out of straw, of which
the Museum of English Rural Life holds many examples. In order
to harvest honey from such a hive, it was common practice
to kill the bees inside.

Put Your Hands Together

Joseph Arch was born in Barford, Warwickshire, and worked as
an agricultural labourer. He became a local Primitive Methodist
preacher and put his skills as an orator to use in the establishment
of the National Agricultural Labourers' Union (1872–1896), the first
successful trade union to be established, of which he was President.
Arch was later elected as a Member of Parliament, the first from
a rural labouring-class background.

Orphan Work

1884 (University Art Collection T267), University of Reading.
Minnie Jane Hardman was a student at the Royal Academy in the
late 19th century.

An orphan work is a creative work for which the rightholder cannot
be traced or is unknown.

While the Earth Remaineth

Amateur 8 mm cinefilm by Wilfred Fisher Wyatt (MERL D DX1914), filmed near Maltby in South Yorkshire.

Foot and Mouth

Documentary film, written and directed by Lindsay Anderson (MERL TR MAFF PH6/1).
The film forms part of The Ministry of Agriculture, Fisheries and Food Film Collection, which comprises 295 educational films on a variety of agricultural subjects available to view on request at the Museum of English Rural Life.

Forceps

Hook, lambing (MERL 61/228/1–3), forceps which appear to have been originally designed for human use. The inscriptions on the inside of the handles read: 'YOUNG // EDINBURGH // FIRST PRIZE AWARDED TO JNO. H. GOODLIFE' and 'YOUNG // EDINBURGH // UNIVERSITY OF ABERDEEN // MIDWIFERY CLASS // SESSION 1893–94'.

Galleries

The quotation on p. 31 is taken from Patrick Kavanagh, 'Self Portrait' (1962).
Wagon, Hereford (MERL 62/64), inscribed 'Thomas Tunks, Holmer, Herefordshire', on the side.

Two Rivers Press has been publishing in and about Reading
since 1994. Founded by the artist Peter Hay (1951–2003),
the press continues to delight readers, local and further afield,
with its varied list of individually designed,
thought-provoking books.

The poems in this collection are set in Janson – a lively
modern revival of a traditional serif typeface with high stroke
contrast and a large x-height to aid legibility. For the headings,
we've used Parisine, a contemporary sanserif, to provide a
counterpoint to the classic feel of Janson, and to distinguish
notes and epigraphs from the poems.